Face the Facts
Child Labor

Kaye Stearman

Raintree

Chicago, Illinois

© 2004 Raintree
Published by Raintree, a division of Reed Elsevier, Inc.
Chicago, Illinois
Customer Service: 888-363-4266
Visit our website at www.raintreelibrary.com

For information, address the publisher:
Raintree, 100 N. LaSalle, Suite 1200, Chicago, IL 60602

Printed and bound in China.
07 06 05 04 03
10 9 8 7 6 5 4 3 2 1

Library of Congress Cataloging-in-Publication Data:

Stearman, Kaye.
  Child labor / Kaye Stearman.
    v. cm. -- (Face the facts)
Includes bibliographical references and index.
Contents: What is child labor? -- Child labor in history -- Child labor today -- Why child labor? -- What is being done? -- How can I help? -- Facts and figures.
  ISBN 0-7398-6848-9 (Library Binding-hardcover) -- ISBN 1-4109-0338-9 (Paperback)
  1. Child labor--Juvenile literature. 2. Child labor--History--Juvenile literature. 3. Child labor--Law and legislation--Juvenile literature. [1. Child labor.] I. Title. II. Series.
  HD6231.S74 2004
  331.3'1--dc21
                              2003002058

Acknowledgments
The publisher would like to thank the following for permission to reproduce photographs:
Pp. 4–5, 6, 18, 24, 31, 42 Mark Henley; p. 7 Paul Quayle/Rex Features; p. 9 Musée Condé/AKG London; p. 10 Lewis W. Hine/AKG London; pp. 11, 15 Lewis W. Hine/Hulton Archive; p. 12 Mary Evans Picture Library; pp. 13, 25 AFP/Popperfoto; p. 14 Fernando Moleres/Panos Pictures; pp. 16–17 Today/Rex Features; p. 19 Jean-Leo Dugast/Panos Pictures; pp. 20–21 Morris Carpenter/Panos Pictures; p. 23 Mark Edwards/Still Pictures; p. 26 Erick Christian Ahounou/Associated Press; p. 27 Gerard and Margi Moss/Still Pictures; pp. 28–29 David Browne/Rex Features; p. 30 Kamal Kishore/Reuters/Popperfoto; pp. 32–33 Imageworks/Topham Picturepoint; pp. 34–35 John Isaac/Still Pictures; pp. 37, 38–39 EPA/Press Association; p. 40 Ron Giling/Still Pictures; p. 41 Joerg Boethling/Still Pictures; p. 43 Peter Barker/Panos Pictures; p. 44 (left) M. Cottingham/Christian Aid/Still Pictures; p. 44 (right) Tim Pannell/Corbis; p. 47 Hartmut Schwarzbach/Still Pictures; p. 48 Ron Giling/Still Pictures.

Cover photograph: Mark Henley.

This text has been checked by UNICEF for factual accuracy, but this is not a UNICEF publication and it does not necessarily reflect the views or policy of UNICEF.

Some words are shown in bold, **like this,** you can find out what they mean by looking in the glossary.

Contents

Childhood and Adulthood

Children work all over the world. This is not a new situation. In the past, most children had to work to ensure their family's survival, and this is still the main reason why children work today. In our own society, many older children work—at home or in part-time jobs after school, on weekends, or during school vacations. Many people feel this is a good thing, because it teaches children about the value of money, helps them learn useful skills, and encourages them to take responsibility. But work is only a small part of life for these young adults. The world of full-time work belongs to adulthood.

When does childhood end and adulthood start? In most countries there are different ages for leaving school, driving a car, marrying, drinking alcohol, voting, and so on. For example, in most U.S. states, a young person can drive at sixteen and vote at eighteen but must wait until twenty-one to drink alcohol legally. And although many countries allow students to leave school at fifteen or sixteen, increasing numbers stay until they are eighteen or nineteen, then go on to further studies.

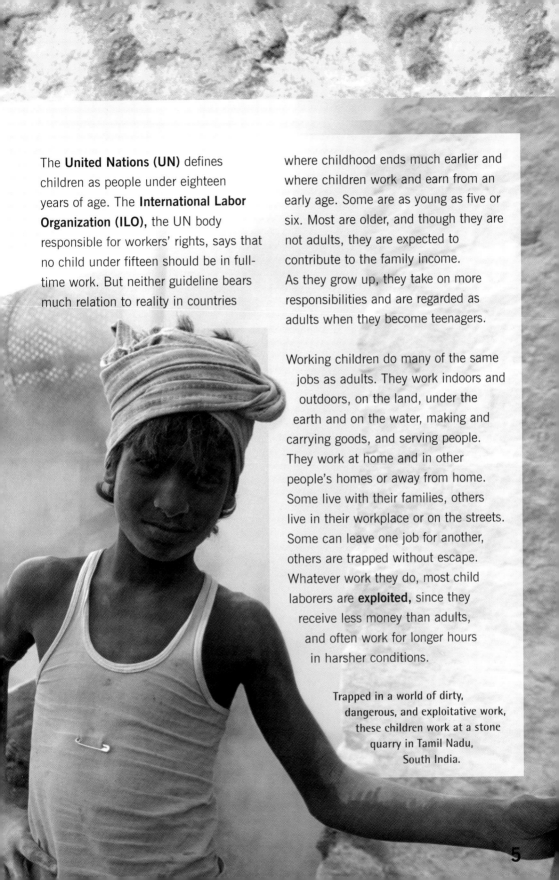

The **United Nations (UN)** defines children as people under eighteen years of age. The **International Labor Organization (ILO),** the UN body responsible for workers' rights, says that no child under fifteen should be in full-time work. But neither guideline bears much relation to reality in countries where childhood ends much earlier and where children work and earn from an early age. Some are as young as five or six. Most are older, and though they are not adults, they are expected to contribute to the family income. As they grow up, they take on more responsibilities and are regarded as adults when they become teenagers.

Working children do many of the same jobs as adults. They work indoors and outdoors, on the land, under the earth and on the water, making and carrying goods, and serving people. They work at home and in other people's homes or away from home. Some live with their families, others live in their workplace or on the streets. Some can leave one job for another, others are trapped without escape. Whatever work they do, most child laborers are **exploited,** since they receive less money than adults, and often work for longer hours in harsher conditions.

Trapped in a world of dirty, dangerous, and exploitative work, these children work at a stone quarry in Tamil Nadu, South India.

5

The Global Picture

No one really knows how many children work on a regular basis. Some governments deny that child labor is a problem or say that numbers are either exaggerated or declining. Others admit that there is a problem but do not know how many children are involved. Working children are often hidden from public view, in homes, factories, and farms.

However, the **ILO** collects statistics and makes regular estimates of the numbers of working children. The results are startling. Worldwide almost 250 million children aged between 5 and 17 (one child in six) are workers, with 179 million (one child in eight) doing jobs that are classified as difficult, dangerous, and unsuitable. This figure does not include normal work around the home, like washing up or cleaning the car, or part-time paid work, like a newspaper route or babysitting. It means working for long hours without a break for wages that are minimal, irregular, or even nonexistent.

So where are these children? Why don't we see them in the everyday world around us? We may know a few of them, although they probably do not attend school regularly and drop out early. But only about one percent of working children come from the wealthy countries of North America, Western Europe, Japan, and Australasia, with another one percent from the former Soviet Union. The remaining 98 percent live in Asia, Africa, Latin America, and the Middle East.

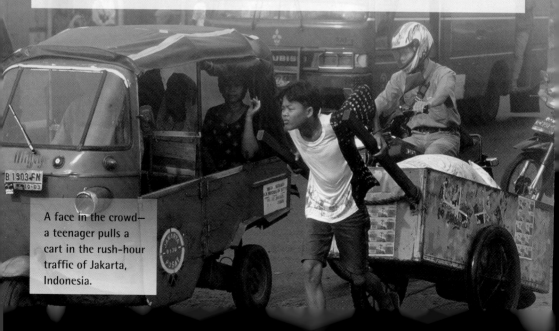

A face in the crowd—a teenager pulls a cart in the rush-hour traffic of Jakarta, Indonesia.

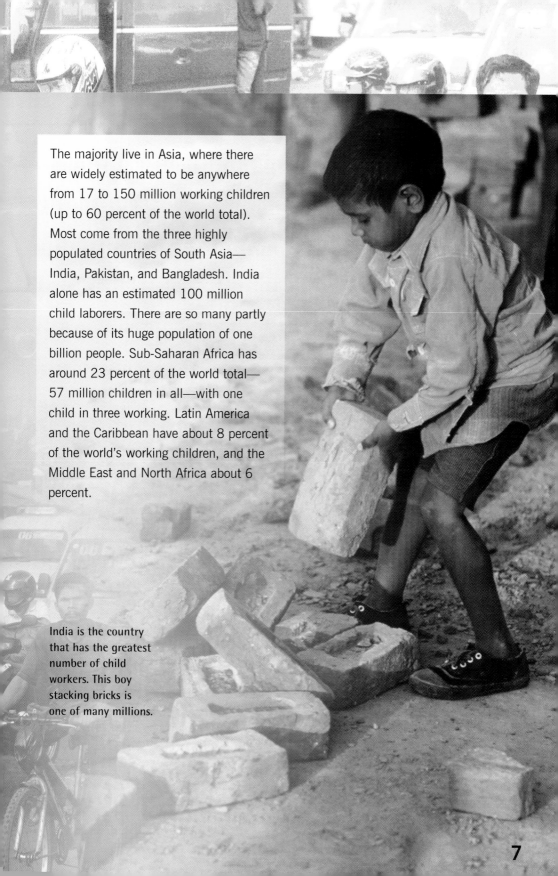

The majority live in Asia, where there are widely estimated to be anywhere from 17 to 150 million working children (up to 60 percent of the world total). Most come from the three highly populated countries of South Asia— India, Pakistan, and Bangladesh. India alone has an estimated 100 million child laborers. There are so many partly because of its huge population of one billion people. Sub-Saharan Africa has around 23 percent of the world total— 57 million children in all—with one child in three working. Latin America and the Caribbean have about 8 percent of the world's working children, and the Middle East and North Africa about 6 percent.

India is the country that has the greatest number of child workers. This boy stacking bricks is one of many millions.

Working for Survival

Until fairly recently, most people had to work simply to survive. In this children were no different from adults. People lived short, active lives and almost everybody worked—but the labor was tailored to an individual's age and skills. Hunting large animals, guiding a heavy plow, or grinding grains were hard and heavy jobs reserved for adults. Children did lighter work such as tending animals, collecting water, and watching their younger brothers and sisters. Even so, they found time to relax and play. As they grew older they took on more difficult work, and by their teenage years were as actively involved in work as adults. In most traditional societies, children followed their parents' occupations, learning from watching and doing rather than from formal occupational schooling.

We know in some societies that children were forced to work too long and far too hard. When archaeologists dug at a site in central Turkey called Catal Hoyuk, they found the remains of many children. Catal Hoyuk was a working community about 8000 years ago, and the presence of so many remains suggests that the children had died of exhaustion from hard work in the surrounding fields. They may have been slaves or children separated from their families.

"Country children in general did not go to school; there were few schools and no reason why they should go to them. . . . The boys would dig the turnips with their father and the girls would reap the corn with their mother. As they all labored together, the older people would talk to the youngsters."

Montaillou—a French village, 1294–1324, Emmanuelle Le Roy Ladurie, 1978

In **medieval** Europe children and adults lived and worked together. From early childhood children wore miniature versions of adult dress. Few went to school or learned to read and write. Most worked from early childhood in the fields or the great houses of the nobility, often for food and lodging rather than money. Childhood was a perilous time. Without modern medicine or knowledge of basic hygiene, many children died at birth or in early childhood. Those who survived had to be tough enough to work and take on adult responsibilities at an early age.

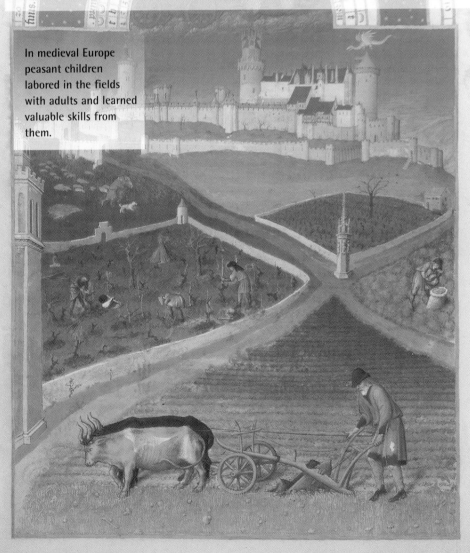

In medieval Europe peasant children labored in the fields with adults and learned valuable skills from them.

The Industrial Revolution

The **Industrial Revolution** began in late 18th-century Britain and was the start of a worldwide change in the way people lived and worked. In the 19th century, it spread to Europe, North America, and parts of Asia.

By introducing machinery powered by the new methods of water and steam, and later, coal and electricity, factory owners were able to increase production dramatically. Skilled jobs were made obsolete and new, less-skilled ones were created. For example, handwoven cloth was replaced by machine-made cloth. Many of the new

Young children, such as this girl, worked in U.S. factories until the early 20th century.

❝The manufacturers begin to employ children rarely of five years, often of six, very often of seven, usually eight to nine years, [and] the working day often lasted fourteen to sixteen hours exclusive of meals and intervals.❞

Frederick Engels, *The Condition of the Working Class in England,* 1845 jobs were filled by children, working for long hours in terrible, often life-threatening, conditions.

The factory system

Even before the rise of large factories, children had worked as **handloom** weavers. But they worked with their families, in their own homes. When demand was high, hours were long, but they did not have to work the same long hours every day. The introduction of large factories employing hundreds of people meant that work was **standardized** and strictly supervised. Workers spent hours doing the same monotonous job. Tiny children were employed to operate and maintain the busy machines because they were smaller and more nimble, and also because they were much cheaper to pay than adults.

In the worst cases, orphaned and abandoned children were "rented out" to factory owners as **"apprentices."** They lived on the factory premises, were given basic food and clothing, and spent all their waking hours at work. The system was so bad that in 1802, the British government passed a law limiting child apprentices in cotton and woollen mills to twelve hours a day and banned night work. It was only in 1847 that British law limited working hours for children and adults to ten hours a day. Meanwhile thousands of children remained working in textile mills, coal mines, and other degrading employment. Many were killed or badly injured. Tiny children were even used as **chimney sweeps**, forced to climb inside tall chimneys thick with soot. It must have been a terrifying experience, alone in the soot and darkness.

Children transport coal in an English coal mine around 1840. In 1842, the British Parliament passed laws prohibiting young children from working in hazardous conditions underground. By 1923 the ban was extended to children under fourteen.

Reforming the Factory System

Not everyone thought that child labor was bad. In Great Britain, factory owners profited from using child laborers and vigorously defended their role. Most people thought that it was normal for poor children to work to add to the family income. After all, it was not as if there was much else available for children. Only better-off people educated their children, either at home or at school. The only schools for the poorest children were part-time day schools or Sunday schools, and these were often badly run.

However, in the early 19th century people began to speak out against the **exploitation** of factory children. Some men who had lost their jobs to children joined the new **trade unions** to improve wages and working conditions.

Reformers, **radical** politicians, **evangelical** ministers, journalists, and writers—even a few progressive factory owners—**campaigned** against child labor. Robert Owen, a textile factory owner in Scotland, established a "model factory" at New Lanark in Scotland that had a childcare facility and a schoolroom for younger children, and light and airy workrooms for older children and adults. Owen's workers were paid fair wages and lived in comfortable houses.

Children work the spinning machines at the Olympian cotton mills of South Carolina in 1900.

Other European countries followed Britain's industrial path, and by the end of the 19th century, the United States was rapidly **industrializing.** Millions of poor people from Europe migrated to U.S. cities where they found work in the cotton mills and metal foundries, in giant garment factories and tiny shops, in the stockyards and on the railroads. Children often worked long hours in appalling conditions for low wages. Japan also industrialized, with factories employing thousands of teenage girls.

Gradually, however, advances in technology resulted in better and faster machinery, operated by skilled adult workers. This meant there were fewer jobs for young children on the factory floor. More children attended school. Trade unions were gaining recognition and campaigned against child labor. With higher wages and more regular incomes, families in industrialized countries began to feel less need to send children to work.

A twelve-year-old "half-timer" in a textile mill in northwest England in 1920. Half-timers worked only half the day and attended school for the remaining hours.

From Past to Present

From the late 19th century onward, there were two factors above all that kept children from the workforce—legal restrictions and compulsory education. In many **industrializing** countries, including Britain and the United States, there had been fierce opposition to the first laws limiting the hours and types of work that children could do and few inspectors to **enforce** the laws. However, with time it became widely accepted that young children needed to be protected from **exploitation,** and that governments could do this through stronger laws and better enforcement. Factories had to be inspected regularly, and bad employers were taken to court and fined for breaking the laws. In practice, some children slipped through the net but, gradually, in industrialized

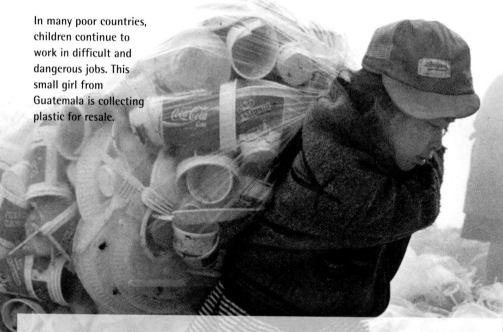

In many poor countries, children continue to work in difficult and dangerous jobs. This small girl from Guatemala is collecting plastic for resale.

❝Child labor remains a problem on a massive scale. . . . The international community still faces a major uphill struggle against this stubbornly pervasive form of work that takes a tragic toll on millions of children around the world.❞

Juan Somavia, Director-General of the ILO (May 2002)

countries the employment of younger children became less common.

So what happened to the children? The answer is simple. Many more were going to school. A changing industrial society meant people needed new skills and these could only come through formal education. Literacy and numeracy were essential for work and everyday tasks. Governments passed laws making elementary and, later, secondary education compulsory, and used taxes to fund state education systems. At the beginning of the 20th century, children in most Western countries stayed in school until the age of twelve or fourteen—low by today's standards but vastly different from even 50 years earlier.

But child labor hasn't disappeared. Today there are more working children than ever in history. Some of these children work in factories in conditions similar to those of the **Industrial Revolution,** but many more are living and working on the land, in small businesses and private homes, and on the streets. Nearly all live in countries where levels of poverty are high, **trade unions** are weak or banned, laws on child labor are nonexistent or not enforced, and education systems are inadequate or nonexistent.

In the United States, as in many other countries, trade unions played an important part in the movement against child labor. This poster from the 1940s was displayed by the Massachusetts United Labor Committee.

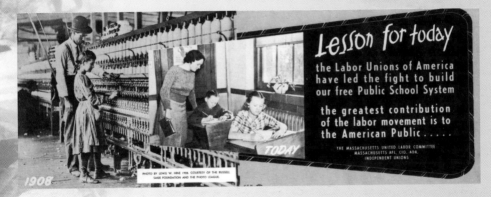

Lesson for today

the Labor Unions of America have led the fight to build our free Public School System

the greatest contribution of the labor movement is to the American Public . . . . .

THE MASSACHUSETTS UNITED LABOR COMMITTEE
MASSACHUSETTS AFL, CIO, ADA,
INDEPENDENT UNIONS

TODAY

1908

PHOTO BY LEWIS W. HINE 1908. COURTESY OF THE RUSSELL SAGE FOUNDATION AND THE PHOTO LEAGUE.

Children in Agriculture

Most working children are found in rural areas, planting, weeding, and harvesting crops, raising animals, catching and cleaning fish, or carrying water. Most of these children work alongside their families, on small farms or large commercial **plantations.** Many children are not full-time workers and some combine light tasks or seasonal work with attending school. Although these children are working, they are not doing tasks that will damage their bodies or their minds.

Yet much agricultural work is dangerous for children. Children may work long hours, spray **pesticides** without wearing protective clothing, and use heavy equipment and dangerous tools. Some are injured or suffer long-term health problems. Some children work far from home and family. The wages paid to children are much lower than those paid to adult workers.

Some of the goods produced by child labor, such as coffee, cocoa, tea, sugar, fruit and vegetables, and fish and seafood, end up on the dinner tables of the rich. Huge competition forces farmers to produce crops ever more quickly and cheaply. What has made things much worse is that the prices paid for these crops have fallen sharply, so the growers try to get cheaper and cheaper labor. That is why so many children pick beans in the coffee plantations of Central America or labor in the sugar fields of Brazil. That is also why teenage boys travel to the cocoa farms of West Africa or dive for shrimp off the coasts of India and Indonesia.

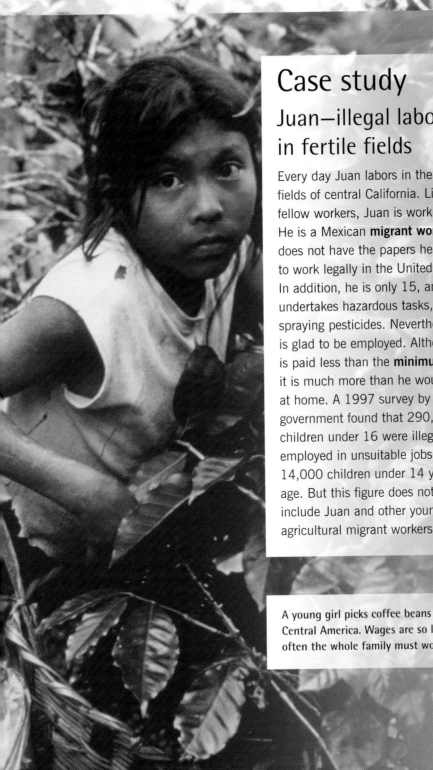

Case study
Juan—illegal labor in fertile fields

Every day Juan labors in the fertile fields of central California. Like his fellow workers, Juan is working illegally. He is a Mexican **migrant worker** who does not have the papers he needs to work legally in the United States. In addition, he is only 15, and he undertakes hazardous tasks, such as spraying pesticides. Nevertheless, Juan is glad to be employed. Although he is paid less than the **minimum wage,** it is much more than he would earn at home. A 1997 survey by the U.S. government found that 290,000 children under 16 were illegally employed in unsuitable jobs, including 14,000 children under 14 years of age. But this figure does not even include Juan and other young agricultural migrant workers.

A young girl picks coffee beans in Nicaragua, Central America. Wages are so low that very often the whole family must work to survive.

Children in Manufacturing

When we think of child workers, we are most likely to think of children laboring for long hours in factories, like those in the early years of the **Industrial Revolution.** Today millions of children continue to work in **manufacturing.** Most are in Asia, but some are found in Europe and the Americas. For example, the **ILO** reports that young teenagers work in the shoe industry in Portugal.

Workshops and factories

Most children who work in manufacturing are found in small workshops, working by hand or using simple machinery. They mainly make goods for sale locally, such as bricks, matches, cigarettes, fireworks, glass ornaments, and locks. Smaller numbers work in large factories, producing goods (such as clothes or shoes) for export. Most do repetitive, unskilled work in poor conditions. Accidents are common and safety regulations are routinely ignored.

Bonded laborers

In South Asia some children become **bonded laborers.** Bonded laborers are people who have borrowed money from an employer and in return agree to work for them until the loan is repaid. Children often work to repay their parents' debts. Child bonded laborers have been discovered in small carpet workshops in northern India and Pakistan. Some work up to twenty hours a day without a break, in tiny, dark rooms. They are deprived of food, are in poor health, and often suffer from eye problems.

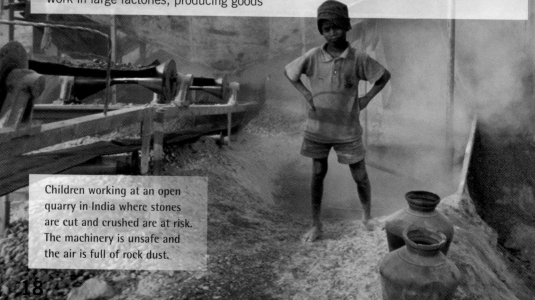

Children working at an open quarry in India where stones are cut and crushed are at risk. The machinery is unsafe and the air is full of rock dust.

Case study
Narsamma—new industry, old practices

Twelve-year-old Narsamma works in the **hybrid** cottonseed industry in Andhra Pradesh state, southern India. Her work, which involves taking each seed apart by hand and **pollinating** it with another seed to make the hybrid, is more like factory work than farming. It is difficult, precise work and it is all done by young girls like Narsamma. For six months a year, Narsamma works from 6:30 in the morning until 7:00 in the evening. She sleeps in a cattle shed, together with dozens of other girls. Narsamma is a bonded laborer who must work to repay a loan her father took out three years ago. Today there are 400,000 girls between seven and fourteen years old working in India's hybrid cottonseed industry. Most of the seeds are bought by Indian or U.S. companies for sale to other farmers.

A boy sorts and packs jeans in a factory in Thailand.

19

Children in Domestic Service

"Child domestic workers are the world's most forgotten children. They may well be the most vulnerable and **exploited** children of all, as well as the most difficult to protect." These are the words of the **United Nations** Children's Fund (UNICEF) in its 1997 annual report on child labor.

One of the largest groups of working children work in **domestic service,** that is, as servants in other people's homes. About 90 percent are girls. There is no accurate estimate of their numbers, and they are largely overlooked. Many are very young, sometimes only five or six years old, and many live far from their families, never seeing them for months or years. Few attend school.

Poor children work as servants for better-off families. Although they are children themselves, they look after children, wash, cook, clean, and serve for incredibly long hours, for small wages or no wages at all. They receive basic food and lodging, often eating leftovers and sleeping on the floor. Some are beaten and abused, physically or sexually. And, whether they are treated well or badly, all lose their childhoods to work.

Where are these child servants? There are millions in South Asia—India, Bangladesh, Pakistan, and Nepal. There are millions more in Africa, Latin America, and Southeast Asia. A few are found in Europe and North America, often teenagers serving wealthy foreign families. But these children are often hidden from sight, so it is difficult to know who they are, where they live, or what their lives are like.

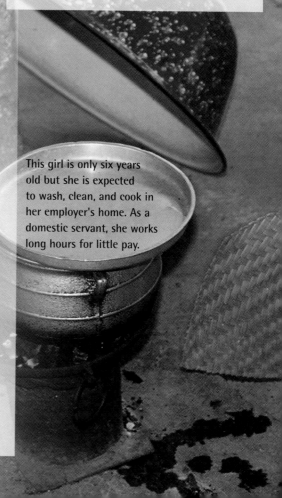

This girl is only six years old but she is expected to wash, clean, and cook in her employer's home. As a domestic servant, she works long hours for little pay.

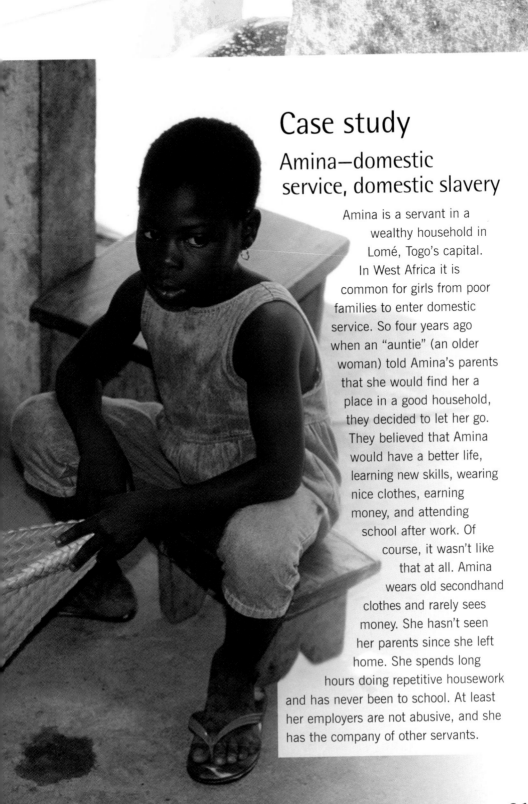

Case study

Amina—domestic service, domestic slavery

Amina is a servant in a wealthy household in Lomé, Togo's capital. In West Africa it is common for girls from poor families to enter domestic service. So four years ago when an "auntie" (an older woman) told Amina's parents that she would find her a place in a good household, they decided to let her go. They believed that Amina would have a better life, learning new skills, wearing nice clothes, earning money, and attending school after work. Of course, it wasn't like that at all. Amina wears old secondhand clothes and rarely sees money. She hasn't seen her parents since she left home. She spends long hours doing repetitive housework and has never been to school. At least her employers are not abusive, and she has the company of other servants.

Children in Shops and Catering

In many countries it is easy to spot children selling goods in markets, in small shops, and on roadsides, or serving customers in tea shops, cafes, restaurants, and hotels. Some are working part-time, before or after school or during school vacations. This situation is fairly common in Western countries, where older children and teenagers help out in family stores and other businesses on a part-time basis. These jobs give children skills and responsibilities as well as money.

However, many children throughout the world are forced to work long hours in very tough conditions. They start early and finish late, and work for hours without a break. In India, for example, it is common to see small boys of seven or eight in restaurants serving customers, clearing tables, and washing dishes late at night. They often live on the premises, far from their families, sleeping on or under tables, and eating leftover food. Like **domestic servants** they may be treated harshly by their bosses. However, if conditions are bad, and they have the freedom to move on, they may leave to look for another job, especially as they get older.

Case study
Ram—long hours, demanding customers

Eleven-year-old Ram works in a big hotel in a tourist town in southern India. His job is to cater to customers, bringing them food and drink when they order it. The hours are long and the customers are often demanding and bad tempered. Nevertheless, Ram enjoys his work and thinks he is lucky. His wages are low, but he gets tips from customers. He has a place to sleep, enough to eat, and time to socialize with the other boys working in the hotel. He has learned a lot about people and the wider world, and can even speak some Hindi and English. When he was younger, Ram worked in a busy city restaurant, where life was much harder. One day he hopes he will have his own restaurant.

Even children in family-owned shops, such as this girl in the Philippines, may find themselves working for hours without a break.

Children on the Streets

Millions of children in **less-developed countries** work on the city streets. Most have families and many live at home or return home regularly. Others spend all their time on the streets, often banded together in gangs for friendship and protection. Working on the streets can be dangerous, especially for children without families.

Street children do many types of work, especially providing services to better-off people—carrying bags, running errands, guarding parked cars, shining shoes, or collecting and sorting trash for resale or recycling. Some beg or steal from passersby. Most have no special skills or equipment, so they learn to become smart and streetwise. They earn very little, and they normally need to spend what they earn each day.

It is nearly always illegal for children to work on the streets, but street children say they have no choice and that it is the only way to survive. Many street children have experienced problems at home such as poverty, violence, or abuse. Some children become separated from their families during wars, riots, or **evictions** and never find their way back home.

Worldwide, boys are more likely to work on the streets than girls, who tend to stay with their families or find work as servants or in factories. But for boys and girls alike, street life is very dangerous. It is common to be cheated, robbed and beaten, run down by cars, or arrested by the police. Some children perform sexual acts for money or become addicted to

A street child sits on the sidewalk outside an expensive shoe shop in Mexico City.

glue, alcohol, or other drugs. Street children in South America have even been killed by police to "clear the streets." In one 1993 incident in Rio de Janeiro, Brazil, police "death squads" killed eight street children. Eight years later, two of the children who had survived the massacre in Rio de Janeiro also met violent deaths at the hands of the police.

A three-year-old girl sells cigarettes on the streets of Jakarta, Indonesia. Her role is as much to attract customers as to make sales.

Case study
Evans—a small child on dangerous streets

In Kenya's capital city, Nairobi, ten-year-old Evans is homeless. He lives and sleeps on the streets of Kibera, Africa's largest slum, with three other boys. Evans has lived like this ever since his home was destroyed in gang fighting. He ran away in the confusion and when he returned, he found that his family had left Kibera. Now his three friends are his family. They share the money they earn through odd jobs or begging. Life on the streets is tough and dangerous, and they often go hungry. Most of all they fear the police and the criminal gangs who control the slums.

Trafficking in Children

Some types of child labor are so extreme that they can be described as slavery. Child **bonded laborers** are one example. Another is child **trafficking,** where children are removed from their home and community by violence or deceit and trapped in situations that they cannot escape from.

Growing numbers of children are bought and sold like slaves and taken far away, often to another country. These illegal activities are organized by ruthless criminal gangs, interested only in profit. Trafficking flourishes in areas of extreme poverty and in countries affected by war and conflict. No one knows how many children are involved.

In April 2001 **UN** officials discovered a ship off the West African coast crammed with young children. They were being transported from Togo and Benin to oil-rich Gabon, in central Africa, to become **domestic servants.** It was not the first time this had happened. There had been previous accounts about the trade in young girls and the terrible conditions they endured on the journey and after their arrival.

There have been similar cases elsewhere. For example, thousands of girls have been trafficked from Nigeria and Albania to Italy, to work on the streets. Young girls are smuggled across borders in Southeast Asia and sold for prostitution. Thousands of children in northern Uganda have been kidnapped by a rebel army. During their captivity, which may last for years, the girls are taken as housekeepers and sexual servants by soldiers, while the boys are forced to become soldiers themselves. It is a horrifying and dangerous life for a trapped and trafficked child.

This young girl faces a bleak future. No one knows how many children have been taken from their families and used as slave labor, unable to escape.

Case study
Ali—a frightened child far from home

Ali is one of hundreds of young "camel jockeys" in the Gulf States. Camel racing is a popular activity there, and small children are considered the best riders. Ali was only five when he was taken from his village in Bangladesh and smuggled into the Gulf States. Now he cannot remember his village, his family, or even his native language. It is a terrifying experience being strapped to a camel racing past the screaming crowds. Some boys are injured or even killed during the races. Although it is now against the law to employ child jockeys, the practice still continues and so does the child trafficking.

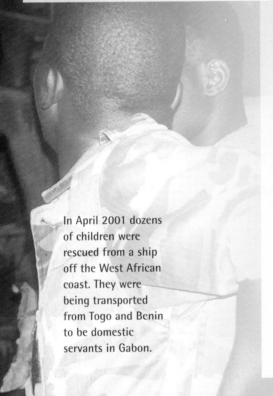

In April 2001 dozens of children were rescued from a ship off the West African coast. They were being transported from Togo and Benin to be domestic servants in Gabon.

27

The Employers' View

Child labor takes many forms. At best, working children are seen as family assets, their work is valued, and they gain skills. At worst, they live like slaves, their work is unpaid, and they receive only basic food and lodging, but no health care or education. Escape is difficult or impossible and they do not know their rights as either children or workers.

Most working children are not slaves, but they are cheap, easy to control, and easy to hire and fire. So it is not hard to see why some employers want to use child labor. This is especially true in industries where technology is simple and competition is fierce. Making handwoven carpets is one example.

Employers sometimes argue that children's tiny fingers are especially adept at weaving complex, tight patterns. But in fact, the most intricate and expensive carpets are made by skilled adult workers. Children tend to work on lower-quality products.

Employers also prefer child labor because children are less able to **strike** or to disrupt production. They are unlikely to know their rights as children or as workers. They find it hard to join **trade unions,** which strive to raise adult wages and are opposed to children working for lower wages. Few working children or their employers are known to government inspectors.

Some employers justify child labor by pointing out that poor children have few alternatives. In other words, they are doing children a favor by employing them and keeping them away from the dangerous streets. Today this argument has little justification as far as the youngest children are concerned. All countries agree that young children should be in school rather than at work. But what about older children who have left school, who want and need to work? Many employers would argue that without legal employment they would be pushed into unsafe jobs or onto the streets.

To some extent this is true. Not all employers are bad. In some cases they have been persuaded to move away from child labor and to give existing child workers time off for schooling. But most changes have resulted from outside pressure. As in the early years of the **Industrial Revolution** in Europe and the United States, employers rarely change of their own free will.

Young girls work in a small match factory in India. Employers prefer children for this work because they are cheap to hire and rarely protest against bad conditions.

29

The Parents' View

Why do some parents send children to work? Some parents are cruel, abusive, or addicted to drugs or alcohol. Others see little value in education and want children to start earning money. In many countries parents have worked since childhood themselves and expect their children to follow the same path. However, the single most important factor is poverty. Children work because their earnings are needed to contribute to the family's income.

For those living in the West (Europe and the United States) it is hard to appreciate the daily difficulties facing poor families in many parts of Asia, Africa, or Latin America. Wages are low and regular jobs are difficult to come by. There are few **benefits** paid by the government, such as child support, unemployment benefits or pensions, or insurance policies to tide people over during difficult times. Health and education are rarely free or low cost, so even the poorest people find themselves having to pay their hospital bills and school fees. Poor people find it hard to pay the high prices charged for basic services such as electricity, water, or garbage collection. The result is that even a child's small wages can make a difference to the family income.

A father and his seven-year-old son work together in a stone quarry near New Delhi, the capital of India.

In some cases, parents may send children away from home to save the expense of feeding and clothing them, as is is the case with many child servants. Often parents believe that this is for everyone's good, that the child will learn new skills, become self-supporting, and one day return to support other family members. In reality, most children gain only misery and abuse from such experiences, and some lose contact with their families forever.

Most families do not want to see their children working long hours. Most would prefer to see them go to school, even if only for a few years. And certainly few would choose to send a small child away from home if alternatives were available. But many families desperately need the extra income. Unless we solve the problem of family poverty, it will be difficult to end child labor.

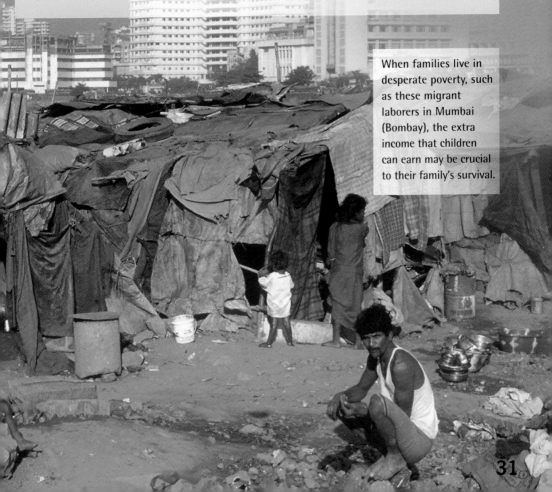

When families live in desperate poverty, such as these migrant laborers in Mumbai (Bombay), the extra income that children can earn may be crucial to their family's survival.

The Children's View

What do children themselves think about having to work? The fact is that it is very difficult to know. Child workers are often hidden from view and they are often frightened to talk to outsiders. Working children may not even know what a different life could offer.

For the youngest children who work in the worst conditions, far from their families, life is very bleak. Many do not understand why their parents sent them away. Most dream of returning home with money or getting a better job with a kinder employer. Many say that they want to play and go to school like other children.

On the other hand, some children say that they are proud to be working and earning. At first they may give their wages to their parents but later many insist on keeping some earnings for themselves. Some children, especially those from violent or unhappy homes, are glad to live independent lives. These children need to be tough and streetwise to survive.

The situation of older children is more complex. In most countries teenagers work part-time, outside of school hours or on weekends, or during school vacations.

In poorer countries many children leave school after elementary level or drop out early. They must work to earn money for themselves and their family to survive. Whatever the law says, governments quietly accept that many older children are working. Banning them from working is usually not effective. Poorly thought-out **campaigns** against child labor can sometimes make things worse.

Some working children are proud of their independence and ability to earn a living. These boys live on the platforms of the largest railroad station in Calcutta (now Kolkata), India.

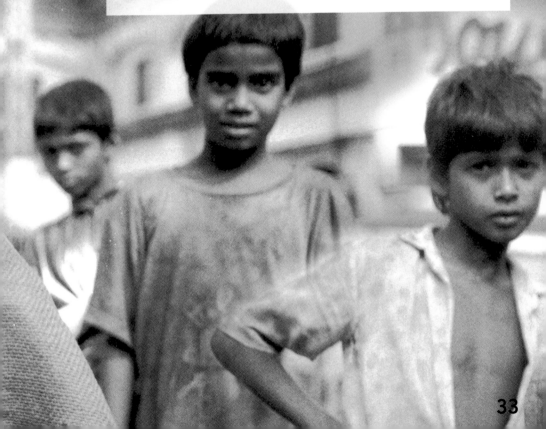

Case study

Clothing factories in Bangladesh

In 1992 **Congress** proposed to stop importing goods made by workers under fifteen years of age. The measure was aimed at clothing factories in Bangladesh, which mainly employed women and girls, some of whom were thirteen or fourteen. Although the girls begged to be allowed to keep their safe, regularly paid jobs, the factories began dismissing the youngest girls. Yet they still needed to work. Some became **domestic servants** or street workers —dangerous and unpleasant jobs. Rather than helping the children, the proposal made their situation worse. Later, it was agreed that the older girls could work full-time, and the younger ones could work part-time while attending school. However, it is difficult to do well at school if you have been working for years.

Does Society Benefit from Child Labor?

Who benefits from child labor? Some people certainly do. Uncaring employers who pay low wages to make extra profits— and abusive parents who exploit their children for gain—both benefit directly from child labor. But what about society as a whole?

Child labor and economic growth

Some **economists** and historians point out that countries in Europe, North America, and Asia used child labor in the early years of **industrialization.** They say that it is rational for **less-developed countries** to use cheap child labor to compete with richer **economies.** Child labor helps to bring about the economic growth that will eventually result in higher living standards. As wages and conditions improve, parents choose to send children to school rather than to work.

Other people argue that there is no proven link between child labor and economic growth. They say that the economies of **more-developed countries** are built on education, skills, finance, and changing technology, not cheap labor. Furthermore, most children do not work in growth industries such as computing or science, but in agriculture, **domestic service,** or on the streets.

Child labor and society

But the economic argument is not the only one. Are there any other benefits for society as a whole from child labor? To become a healthy adult, a child needs good food, fresh air, space to play, and opportunities to learn. These are not possible if children spend long hours at work in bad conditions. Instead their bodies become stunted, their eyes and ears are damaged by poor light or loud noise, and their minds receive no stimulation. Many working children have little or no schooling and never learn to read and write. Some are killed or badly injured at work. Some are physically or sexually abused or are removed from their families, perhaps never to return. Many are forced to grow up fast, accepting adult responsibilities for younger children when they are still children themselves. Most people argue that, under such circumstances, neither children nor society as a whole benefit from child labor.

Some children work in export industries, such as this carpet factory in India. But does society as a whole benefit from child labor?

Laws Against Child Labor

There are few governments today that openly support child labor. Many have banned it completely or restrict it to family farms or family businesses. Every country, except the United States and Somalia, has signed the **UN Convention** on the Rights of the Child, an agreement that lists children's human rights. (The United States feel that it can support children without signing the Convention.) Over 130 countries, including the United States, have signed Convention 182 of the **ILO,** which calls for immediate action against the worst forms of child labor.

But while passing laws and signing international conventions is relatively easy, putting them into action can be very difficult. Governments need to appoint inspectors and retrain police officers and civil servants to act against offending employers. They must convince parents to send children to school rather than to work. Some governments simply do not have the skills or capacity to **enforce** the laws. Many governments lack the will to act and many are corrupt. Many governments act in favor of employers rather than children. The fact is that employers have money, influence, and votes; children have none of these.

In India, with 100 million child workers, the government has signed over 120 ILO Conventions, all seeking to end child labor, including **bonded labor.** Yet child labor is widespread and openly acknowledged. Between 1986 and 1993, 4,000 employers of children were brought before a court. Only a quarter were found guilty and not one went to jail. Many of the politicians who pass laws to protect children, and the judges and police who enforce them, have child servants at home and pass working children in the streets every day.

A few governments take no action against child labor, and some even use it themselves. In Myanmar hundreds of thousands of people have been forced to work for the army, without pay and in terrible conditions. Despite government denials, observers say that children are used as porters, messengers, and laborers, and are worked in the same brutal way as adults.

A boy in Bamako, Mali, displays a "Red Card Against Child Labor." The cards were distributed by the International Labor Organization at an African soccer tournament.

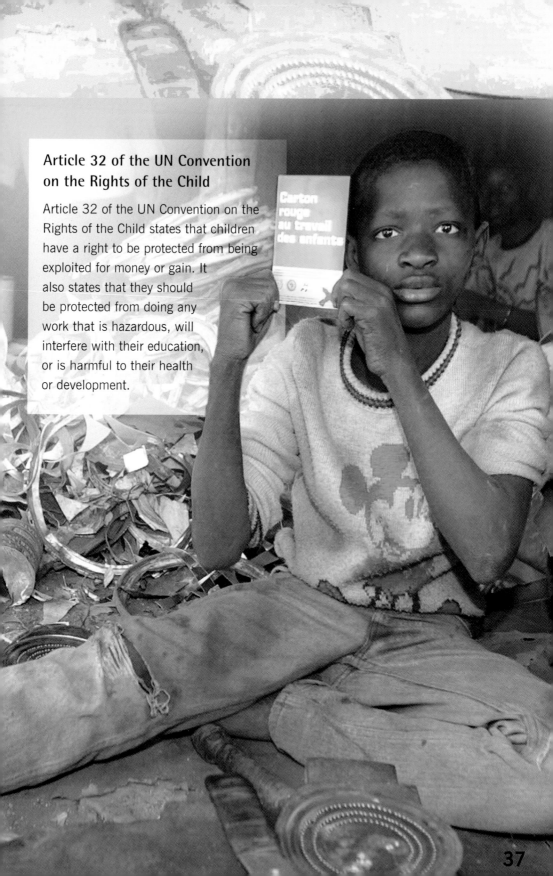

Article 32 of the UN Convention on the Rights of the Child

Article 32 of the UN Convention on the Rights of the Child states that children have a right to be protected from being exploited for money or gain. It also states that they should be protected from doing any work that is hazardous, will interfere with their education, or is harmful to their health or development.

Organizing Against Child Labor

In the 19th century, opposition to child labor came from organizers who wrote pamphlets, led demonstrations, and **lobbied** governments. Today the driving force against **exploitation** of children comes from **activists** for children's and workers' rights. The difference is that today's struggles take place on a worldwide stage.

Nongovernmental organizations

In many countries opposition to child labor comes from independent groups known as **nongovernmental organizations (NGOs)**. These range from small local groups to national organizations and international **coalitions.** Some carry out research and publish articles, some organize demonstrations and campaigns. Others give practical assistance to working children by providing meals, shelter, education, and support. Some act to rescue children from **bonded labor** or **trafficking**, cruel employers, or dangerous workplaces.

Trade unions

Trade unions can also play an important role. While they rarely recruit children as members, they may support children in other ways. They call for increases in adult wages so that families are less likely to send children to work to provide extra income. However, the impact of trade unions is limited because many governments ban or restrict trade unions, and many employers act ruthlessly to suppress union activity.

Working children join a demonstration against child labor in New Delhi, India's capital. They are calling on the government to take action to assist working children.

Demonstrations and boycotts

NGOs, **consumer** groups, and trade unions in wealthy countries have sometimes demonstrated against child labor in **less-developed countries,** especially where goods made by children seem to threaten local jobs or industries. Demonstrations and **boycotts** targeted against child labor can be effective. They may force importers to look more carefully at the farms and factories that supply their goods, and take steps to raise wages and improve conditions. However, this may lead to working children being thrown out of their jobs and onto the streets. NGOs, consumer groups, and trade unions may help to improve the lives of some working children, but there are millions more they cannot reach. This is because they cannot solve the underlying problems of poverty that push children into work. That has to be the task of governments and the **UN.**

❝While millions of children are working, millions of adults are unemployed or do not earn enough to make a living. That is why we are convinced that one way to stop child labor is to ensure that their parents have access to decent jobs, decent wages, and that their right to join and form unions is respected.**❞**

Bill Jordan, General Secretary of the International Confederation of Free Trade Unions (ICFTU)

Education to End Child Labor

One of the key factors in ending child labor is providing more and better education. If children attend school, they cannot be working full-time. Children who receive a good education grow up to have more skills that can earn them more income. But this means that families and communities must value education and be prepared to keep children in school rather than send them to work.

These lessons come from history and from the present day. One of the most striking examples is that of India. In Kerala state, in southern India, education is taken very seriously. Every child attends school and almost everyone can read. Only one child in a hundred is working. In Bihar, in the north, education is not so highly valued and the schools are poorly equipped and poorly run. Many children drop out of school early and never learn to read and write. In Bihar, one child in eight is working.

Why don't more children in places like Bihar go to school? There are many reasons. Older children stay at home to look after younger brothers and sisters while parents work. In some places there are no schools. Other schools hardly function, lacking books, desks, or even the simplest equipment. Teachers go

unpaid and classes are huge; 60 or 80 children to a classroom is not uncommon. For many families the biggest single problem in the short run is poverty—even if they want to, they cannot afford to educate their children. Many governments charge fees for elementary and secondary schools. On top of that, there are costs for books, pens and paper, uniforms, and shoes. Making education affordable is vital.

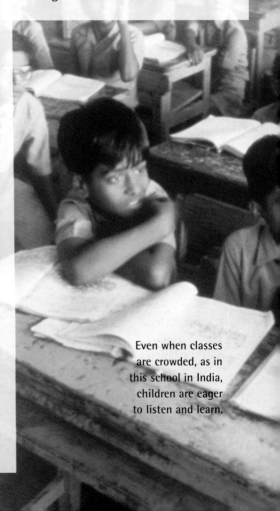

Even when classes are crowded, as in this school in India, children are eager to listen and learn.

In Uganda, the government was able to abolish elementary school fees, enabling hundreds of thousands of poor children to go to school. But expansion has produced further problems. Uganda's schools are bursting at the seams and not all education is good quality.

Primary education for all

Worldwide 130 million children aged 6 to 11 do not attend school; of these 80 million, roughly 60 percent are girls. Millions more children drop out of school early. Elementary education for all children is one of the **UN Millennium Development Goals,** a set of targets to halve poverty by 2015.

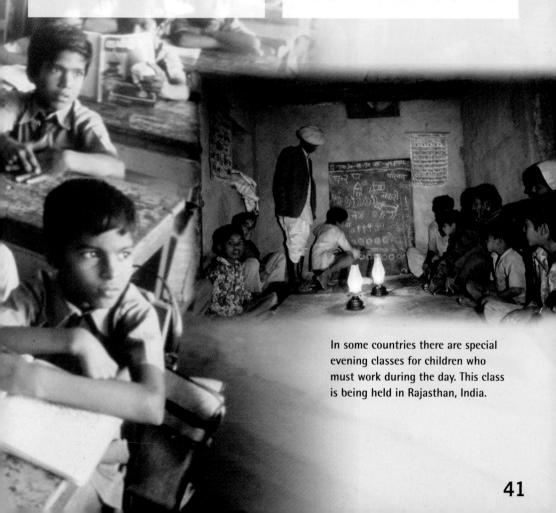

In some countries there are special evening classes for children who must work during the day. This class is being held in Rajasthan, India.

Ending Poverty to End Child Labor

"We must move children to the center of the world's agenda. We must rewrite strategies to reduce poverty so that investments in children are given priority.**"**

Nelson Mandela, former president of South Africa, 2002

Girls in Vietnam carry water, a regular domestic chore. When families have easy access to safe running water, children will be freed of such tasks.

Child labor is directly related to poverty. To end child labor, we need to end poverty. This is a massive task and poses the greatest challenge of our times. Poor countries need jobs and businesses, trade, and **aid.** Poor children need families with secure homes, regular incomes, and flourishing communities with schools and services, such as water and electricity. They need a real childhood of play, school, and home, not long hours of work.

Sometimes simple changes can make a huge difference. Over a billion people lack clean, running water at an affordable price. Almost everywhere water collection is the responsibility of women and girls. If they have to walk for miles or wait for hours to collect water, women cannot do more productive work and girls cannot attend school. And if they must pay a high price for water, they are pushed further into poverty. So providing access to a

Ending extreme poverty and hunger

About 1.2 billion people—one in five of the world's population—live in extreme poverty on less than $1 a day; 2.4 billion live on less than $2 a day. Ending extreme poverty and hunger is one of the **UN Millennium Development Goals,** a set of targets to halve poverty by 2015.

Child labor and poverty exist hand in hand. Providing good housing, clean water and a healthy environment will give children a better life.

safe, cheap water supply can help to reduce poverty and free children from hours of hard labor.

Despite the obstacles, some governments have made real strides in removing children from the fields and factories. For example, in Vietnam, the government has helped the poorest families to improve their standard of living and send their children to school. As a result, in the five years from 1993 to 1998, the numbers of working children fell by 28 percent.

However, for every country that makes progress, others slip back. Wars and conflicts destroy families and communities, pushing children into work or even forcing them into armies. Millions of children have been orphaned by **HIV/AIDS** and have had to manage the best they can. Global action to end poverty is needed to make a difference.

Child Labor and You

What are the links between your life and the lives of the working children described in this book? They seem to be two different worlds. But look closer and explore ways that you can make a difference to their lives.

Do some digging

Learn about the countries where child labor is a problem and speak to people in your own community to find out if child **exploitation** is a problem close to home. Find out about the companies that are likely to employ children. Be prepared to ask for more information if you think that a product is made by children. Write to the company, asking about wages, conditions, and the minimum age of employment. Also ask if their factories are inspected, who does this, and how often. Be persistent. Many companies will not want to answer your questions.

A blind eleven-year-old Indian girl stitches a soccer ball. The balls sell for high prices in Europe.

Look at the label

Some industries where child labor is widely used now label products made without child labor. For example, carpets produced without using child workers now carry a special "rugmark" label.

Pay a fair price

Products, such as coffee and chocolate marked with the "fair-trade" label, pay producers well, and come from farms that do not use child labor. These products can be found in specialty grocery stores.

Write to your representative

Contact the person who represents you in government—your senator or representative in **Congress.** Explain why you are concerned about working children and ask what your government is doing to end child labor worldwide. For example, are they helping poor countries to improve education or take children out of hazardous work? Are they taking action against **traffickers** of children or companies that exploit children?

Give practical support

There are many good **campaigns** to improve the lives of working children and groups that need your support. You could volunteer your time and collect funds for projects such as building day shelters, schools, and training centers for working children. Often a small amount of money can do great things. You can support working children directly through groups such as the Global March Against Child Labor or Kids Can Free the Children.

Remember the day

The **ILO** has declared June 12 of every year World Day Against Child Labor. What actions can you take?

Happy, healthy children on the soccer field. But did other children stitch the ball and sew their outfits?

Children Paying the Price

Look on the shelves of your local store. Some of the items you see will have been produced by child labor. The **ILO** says that child workers are involved in growing crops such as cocoa, tea, coffee, cotton, and rubber.

Take chocolate as an example. Chocolate is made from cocoa, and 70 percent of the world's cocoa is grown in the Ivory Coast, Ghana, and Nigeria in western Africa. The work is hard, conditions are poor, and wages are low. Most of the workers are young men and boys, including 284,000 children. Some workers just get basic food and lodging. The harvested cocoa is bought by big companies and shipped to Western countries (Europe and the United States) where it is turned into chocolate for sale. Yet only a tiny part of the price paid by **consumers** goes to the growers and workers. Much more goes into production, packaging, and distribution, and into profits for the retailer. The price paid to growers for cocoa has fallen sharply in recent years, so workers' wages have fallen even further.

This unfair situation has been highlighted by **activists** who point out that if companies paid higher prices for cocoa, and consumers paid higher prices for chocolate, then workers could receive higher wages. Living standards would rise and parents could afford to send children to school, rather than to work. In May 2002 chocolate manufacturers, human rights groups, and the Ivory Coast government signed an agreement to try to end child labor on cocoa farms by 2005. Some chocolate manufacturers now pledge to pay a higher price for "fair trade" cocoa that comes from farms that do not employ children.

Boys pick tea leaves in Rwanda. If consumers paid higher prices for tea, wages would be higher and children would not need to work.

46

Case study

Habib—hard work, heavy loads

Thirteen-year-old Habib works on a cocoa plantation in the Ivory Coast. The work is hard. Young boys wield long, sharp knives and carry heavy loads. Habib arrived here with a group of boys from his village in Mali. It has become a well-worn trail; Mali is much poorer than the Ivory Coast and many Malians seek work there. Yet Habib has never drunk a cup of cocoa or eaten a bar of chocolate. They are produced in factories overseas. Even if they were available, Habib would never be able to afford them.

Ending Child Labor

Strong laws, active **campaigning** organizations, good schools, secure family incomes, growing **economies**— all have played a part in freeing children from the burdens and dangers of working. Today it is widely accepted that no young child should have to work outside the home and no child should ever have to do dangerous work.

Will we ever really end child labor? With almost 250 million children working worldwide, it is an enormous task. Millions of children must work to earn income and have no opportunity to attend school. Yet there are reasons for hope. Today, most of the world's children regularly attend elementary school and many go on to high school and college. These children do not need to spend their childhood working.

The key to stopping child labor is to end extreme poverty in the communities where children have to work. Poverty is much more than just lack of money. It means lack of choices as well. It means people are forced to live hand to mouth, rather than thinking about longer-term goals such as education, training, and careers. So what is the world doing?

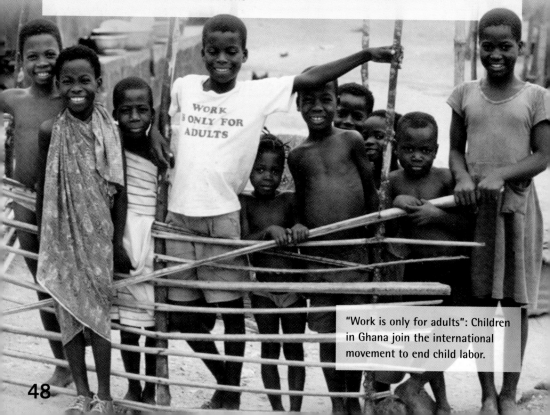

"Work is only for adults": Children in Ghana join the international movement to end child labor.

In September 2000, at the start of the new millennium, the **UN** adopted eight **UN Millennium Development Goals,** a set of targets to cut poverty in half by 2015. If the goals are achieved, they will make a huge difference to working children.

The goals are:

1 End extreme poverty and hunger.

2 Ensure an elementary education for every child.

3 Give equal treatment for girls and boys.

4 Reduce deaths of babies and young children.

5 Improve the health of mothers.

6 Combat **HIV/AIDS,** malaria, and other diseases.

7 Protect the environment.

8 Work in partnership for development.

A few months later, in April 2001, UNICEF, the UN's children's organization, launched the Global Movement for Children. It called on all countries to adopt ten simple pledges to support the rights of all children.

1 Leave no child out.

2 Put children first.

3 Care for every child.

4 Fight HIV/AIDS.

5 Stop harming and **exploiting** children.

6 Listen to children.

7 Educate every child.

8 Protect children from war.

9 Protect the Earth for children.

10 Fight poverty: Invest in children.

Eight goals, ten pledges, dozens of international conventions, thousands of laws worldwide—can they really make a difference to working children? Are they calls to action for a better future, or empty promises? What do you think?

Facts and Figures

Children ages 5–14 in child labor

Region	Numbers	Percentage
Asia and the Pacific	127,300,000	60.5%
Sub-Saharan Africa	48,000,000	23.0%
Middle East and North Africa	13,400,000	6.5%
Latin America and the Caribbean	17,400,000	8.0%
Eastern Europe and former U.S.S.R.	2,400,000	1.0%
Richest countries (in North America, in Western Europe, Japan, Australia)	2,500,000	1.0%
Total	211,000,000	100%
Total children ages 5–17 in work	246,000,000	

Children in work classified as hazardous

5–14 years old: 111,000,000

15–17 years old: 59,000,000

Total 5–17 years old:

170,000,000

Children in slavery

(**bonded labor**, **trafficking**, child soldiers, etc.)

5–17 years old: 8,400,000

Source: A Future Without Child Labor,
International Labor Organization, 2002

Work done by child workers

Type of work	Percentage
Agriculture, fishing, forestry	70.4%
Manufacturing	8.3%
Retail, shops, and catering	8.3%
Domestic and other service	6.5%
Transport and communications	3.8%
Construction	1.9%
Mining and quarrying	0.8%

Source: A Future Without Child Labor,
International Labor Organization, 2002

Going to school

Region	Children attending elementary school		Children attending secondary school	
	Girls	Boys	Girls	Boys
South Asia	68%	74%	33%	52%
East Asia and the Pacific	95%	95%	60%	66%
Sub-Saharan Africa	54%	58%	22%	28%
Middle East and North Africa	76%	84%	55%	64%
Latin America and the Caribbean	92%	92%	53%	49%
Eastern Europe and former U.S.S.R.	80%	82%	82%	82%

Source: UNICEF, The State of the World's Children 2002

International conventions related to child labor

1926	League of Nations Slavery Convention
1930	League of Nations Forced Labor Convention
1948	UN Universal Declaration of Human Rights
1973	ILO Convention 138 (Minimum Age Convention)
1990	UN Convention on the Rights of the Child
1999	ILO Convention 182 (Elimination of the Worst Forms of Child Labor)

"AIDS orphans"

The rapid growth of **HIV/AIDS** in Africa has created millions of "AIDS orphans." As parents and adult relatives die, grandparents and children have to take on the burden of supporting the family. AIDS orphans find themselves digging and hoeing the ground, walking miles each day for water, and looking after younger children—tiring tasks for an adult, let alone a child. All of this is done while trying to come to terms with the loss of his or her parents. Most of these children say that they feel helpless and fear for the future.

Further Information

Contacts in the United States and Canada

Child Labor Coalition
c/o National Consumers League
1701 K Street, NW, Suite 1200
Washington, DC 20006
e-mail: nclncl@aol.com
www.nclnet.org/clc.htm

Fields of Hope (for child agricultural laborers worldwide)
e-mail: info@fieldsofhope.org
www.fieldsofhope.org

International Labor Organization (Washington office)
1828 L Street NW # 600
Washington, DC 20036
email: washilo@ilowbo.org
http://us.ilo.org/ilokidsnew/

Rugmark Foundation
733 15th Street, NW, Suite 912
Washington, DC 20005
e-mail: info@RUGMARK.org
www.rugmark.org

US Fund for UNICEF
333 East 38th Street
New York, NY 10016
e-mail: webmaster@unicefusa.org
www.unicefusa.org/

UNICEF Canada
Canada Square
2200 Yonge Street, Suite 1100
Toronto, ON M4S 2C6
e-mail: secretary@unicef.ca
www.unicef.ca

Kids Can Free The Children
Suite 300, 7368 Yonge Street
Thornhill, Ontario, L4J 8H9
e-mail: info@freethechildren.com
www.freethechildren.org

The Internet

LearningChannel.org
www.learningchannel.org

Global March Against Child Labour
http://globalmarch.org/

NGO Committee on UNICEF
www.ngosatunicef.org

OneWorld (linking 950 organizations)
www.oneworld.net/

United Nations Children's Fund (UNICEF)
www.unicef.org

Further reading

Gay, Kathryn. *Child Labor: A Global Crisis.*
Brookfield, Conn.: Millbrook, 1998.

Haley, James. *Work.* Farmington Hills,
Mich.: Gale Group, 2002.

Stalcup, Brenda. *The Industrial Revolution.*
Farmington Hill, Mich.: Gale Group, 2002.

Williams, Mary E. *Child Labor and
Sweatshops.* Farmington Hill, Mich.: Gale
Group, 1998.

Glossary

activist one who works toward accomplishment of a social goal in the face of opposition

aid funds or supplies, such as food or medicine, given by richer countries to poorer countries

apprentice young person training to do a job

benefits payments made by governments to people who are unemployed, ill, or disabled

bonded laborers people working for others to pay off a debt, often for years and in harsh, dangerous conditions

boycott refusal to buy or handle goods as a punishment or protest

campaign to work toward a goal in an organized way

chimney sweep person who cleans chimneys

coalition group of countries or organizations that join together for a common cause

Congress law-making body of the United States government

consumer person who buys or uses goods or services

convention legal agreement between nations

domestic service work performed by servants in a household

economist expert in economics

economy goods, services, and technology produced by a society

enforce to make sure that people comply with something, such as a law, usually with force or with the threat of fines

evangelical form of Christianity inspired directly by the Bible and especially concerned with converting non-Christians

eviction order by authorities or a private landlord to leave an area or building

exploitation having people work very hard in poor conditions and paying them little or nothing, to make large profits

handloom weaving machine worked by hand

HIV/AIDS Human Immuno-deficiency Virus infection, leading to AIDS (Acquired Immune Deficiency Syndrome), an illness that destroys the body's protective systems

hybrid offspring of two different varieties that have been bred together to produce desirable characteristics

industrialization process of changing from an economy based on agriculture to one based on manufacturing

Industrial Revolution shift from an agricultural to a machine-driven manufacturing economy, usually referring to Britain (1760–1830) and, later, the United States (1877–1914)

International Labor Organization (ILO) UN organization concerned with the conditions and rights of workers

less-developed countries poor, usually agricultural countries trying to raise living standards

lobby try to influence, especially into taking politically significant action

manufacturing making goods on a large scale using machinery

medieval of the Middle Ages in Europe (approximately 500–1500 C.E.)

migrant worker person who travels to work in another area or country. Typically, migrant workers follow the various growing seasons in a given area.

minimum wage lowest level of wages, set by government

more-developed country wealthy, economically and technologically advanced country

nongovernmental organization (NGO) not-for-profit organization with the aim of helping people

pesticide chemical used to kill insects that feed on crops. Pesticides are often hazardous to people and the environment.

plantation large farm, usually growing one crop for sale and worked by laborers

pollinating fertilizing a plant with pollen

radical person with strong political views related to social reform

reformer person who wants to make improvements and remove faults in society

standardized carried out so that products meet a certain quality and size

strike refuse to work in order to win increased pay or better conditions

trade union group of workers joining together to improve wages or conditions

trafficking removing people by force or deceit from their community and (sometimes) selling them, often in another country

United Nations (UN) international organization linking, and working for, all countries of the world

UN Millennium Development Goals targets to halve world poverty worldwide by 2015, including having all children attend elementary school

Index